PRAYERS *For My* MARRIAGE

40 Days of Guided Prayer for Divine Covering, Grace, and Relationship Renewal

STEPHAN LABOSSIERE

Prayers For My Marriage – *40 Days of Guided Prayer for Divine Covering, Grace, and Relationship Renewal*

Published by Highly Favored Publishing

First Edition: December 2018

For information, contact Highly Favored Publishing – highlyfavoredent@gmail.com

Editor & Creative Consultant: C. Nzingha Smith

Formatting: Ya Ya Ya Creative – www.yayayacreative.com

ISBN No. 978-0-9980189-2-8

PRINTED AND BOUND IN THE UNITED STATES OF AMERICA

TABLE OF CONTENTS

INTRODUCTION

Only God is all-knowing. God knows you and God knows your spouse. He also knows what you need to do, specifically, in your marriage to see your union blessed, happy, and thriving. God will empower and direct you in the areas and actions you must take to strengthen your marriage when you seek Him.

Throughout the Bible there are countless examples of ways that God uses people to change the actions of others. He equips us with the tools, knowledge, and wisdom needed to affect change. However, He also requires our participation.

It's ultimately up to you. You must seek God. Then, you need to be obedient to God's instructions and DO what He says to receive the promises of His word.

Prayer works when you are willing to work with your prayers.

So, you see, faith by itself isn't enough.
Unless it produces good deeds, it is dead and useless.
Don't you remember that our ancestor Abraham
was shown to be right with God by his actions
when he offered his son Isaac on the altar?
You see, his faith and his actions worked together.
His actions made his faith complete.
–James 2:17, 21-22

Another example of faith and works being complete is the story of Moses and Pharaoh. Moses sought God for instructions. God gave Moses specific instructions to follow and words to say that resulted in Pharaoh's heart hardening and the release of the Israelites from slavery. The emphasis here is often put on God changing Pharaoh's heart. However, God didn't change his heart. Moses' obedience to God's instructions caused the chain of events that allowed the miracle to happen.

Prayer allows you to receive God's instructions for your life and marriage. God communicates to you what YOU need to do, you follow directions. The result: a chain of events occurs, which allows the miracle of transformation to happen. God equips you through prayer with the power and ability to do the work, which will ultimately lead to the outcome that aligns with His will.

It's a process. You must be a willing instrument that participates from a place of love and with the right attitude.

We have the habit of viewing God as a magician, who will swoop in, wave his hand, and change everything we're praying for — in an instant —to what we want it to be. Unfortunately, this is not how it works. Normally, what we want to change about others, God uses to change us. As a result, our prayers are answered. Not because the other person is new and improved, but because God gives us actions to take that unlock what is needed to improve the situation.

Know that God loves you. He has richly blessed you through the union of your marriage. He wants you happily married. No matter how much you might think you know what's best for you and your spouse, God knows better.

During this 40-day prayer journey, you are going to begin by getting into the right posture before

God. This will ensure you'll be able to receive, what you need, to do your part.

What do I mean by "right posture," you ask? God is a God of order. There is a proper order to everything. If you've read the companion books, *How to Get a Man to Cherish You if You're His Wife* and *How to Get a Woman to Sleep with You if You're Her Husband*, then the idea of submission won't be such a foreign concept.

As a married couple, your first act of submission is to God. We will start there. This way, God will be able to begin to instruct you on the actions you need to take to change your hearts, individually and collectively as a unit. There are some things that keep us in behaviors or in wrong-thinking that hinder us from experiencing the fullness of God's and our spouse's love.

The crazy thing is that we might not even be aware of the things that are keeping us bound. That's why it's so important to allow God to take the lead over your life and your marriage.

Once you're resubmitted to God and each other, God can begin to teach you how to correct your hearts and check your attitudes. You will then have more room to free your marriage from the bondage of unforgiveness, malice, resentment, anger, and sin, which are seeds of unhappiness.

In the latter part of the book, you'll focus on praying for guidance for better communication with each other. This includes, freely expressing and receiving the love you desire to experience in your marriage.

Finally, you'll focus your prayers and actions on God's gift to you as a married couple: uninhibited intimacy both sexual and non-sexual.

OPENING PRAYER

God I intercede and pray on behalf of the married couple reading this book at this right time in their lives. They're seeking you as the foundation for which they want the grace and favor to begin anew in their marriage.

God, thank you for your eternal and unconditional love for them. Help them to believe it's not too late and that you are the God of second, third, and fiftieth chances.

God, your grace is sufficient for them throughout this 40-day journey to uninhibited love with one another and a strengthened relationship. You are the God of miracles, signs, and wonders working through us. Show up mighty in their lives and in their marriage right now.

It's your power in them that will allow them to free themselves of old patterns of behavior that no longer serve their union nor honor you. Help them to learn to lean on you for direction in everything concerning their marriage. Help them to believe in themselves and their ability to be good spouses to each other.

I serve notice to the devil right now that he has no power nor place within the sanctity of that which you have joined together for your honor and glory. Help this couple get back to a place where they are honoring you with and in their union.

I believe that you will help them transform their minds, renew their hearts, redeem their time, and give them a refreshing new foundation of what it means to be married. Over the next 40 days, as they listen to your instructions and take the steps needed to make it happen, I thank you in advance for your faithfulness toward them.

You are not a respecter of persons and you don't operate on our timetable, so I pray they will trust you to move in their lives and marriage in your perfect timing.

I believe you've heard my prayer, God, and that you will honor it.

By faith, I declare it done and so, in Jesus name, *Amen.*

THE GIFT OF *Submission*

DAY 1

REFLECTION

Ultimately, God should be the leader in your marriage. God is not going to let you down. He's not going to forsake you, even when your spouse does.

He's not going to let your efforts be in vain. Even when your efforts don't produce the results you're looking for right away. Everything will work in God's timing and for your good.

SCRIPTURE STUDY

So, humble yourselves before God,
resist the devil and he will flee from you.
–James 4:7

PRAYER

Heavenly Father, forgive us, for we know not what we do.

As a unit, we repent and ask for your forgiveness for not putting you first in our lives and in our marriage.

We seek to get back in right alignment with your will for our lives and our union.

By faith, it is so, in Jesus name, *Amen*.

DAY 2

REFLECTION

God will lead your marriage in the direction it's supposed to go. If you honor Him, God will honor you.

God is faithful even when you're not.

Let God have the final say and let Him guide you and the decisions in your marriage and you can't go wrong.

SCRIPTURE STUDY

We know how much God loves us, and we have put our trust in his love. God is love, and all who live in love live in God, and God lives in them.
–1 John 4:16

PRAYER

God, we come to you now with open hearts and in a posture of humility. We desire to submit to your leadership in our marriage.

Your ways are higher than ours, God. Although we might not understand, by faith, we will trust that you know what's best for our lives.

God, teach us how to trust you with everything concerning our lives, our love, our relationship, each other, our home, and our finances.

By faith, it is so, in Jesus name, *Amen.*

DAY 3

REFLECTION

God's guidance is the key
to changing your situation.

God will tell you exactly what you
need to do in your marriage.

Don't assume you know what's best.
Your knowledge is limited.

You don't know better than God.

SCRIPTURE STUDY

Most of all, let love guide your life, for then the whole church will stay together in perfect harmony.
–Colossians 3:14

PRAYER

God, teach us how to release our need to be in control. We need your direction and guidance for our lives and marriage. We don't have all the answers and we're tired of trying things that don't last.

We no longer want the responsibility that comes with being in control. We admit that it's too much for us to handle.

You are all-knowing. Thank you, God, for being enough. We seek to love and honor you.

By faith, it is so, in Jesus name, *Amen*.

DAY 4

REFLECTION

Understand that this a process and everything won't change overnight. With that said, I want to remind you that your spouse and your marriage are blessings from God. You have a responsibility to honor the blessing God has entrusted you with.

SCRIPTURE STUDY

In the same way, you husbands must give honor to your wives. Treat your wife with understanding as you live together. She may be weaker than you are, but she is your equal partner in God's gift of new life. Treat her as you should so your prayers will not be hindered.

1 Peter 3:7

PRAYER

God, we desire to learn how to submit to your will and your leadership for our marriage. Teach us how to be patient with ourselves and each other during this process.

Help us to mature in our faith so that we won't have a need for immediate gratification and won't be easily discouraged when we can't see how things are going to turn out.

"Now faith is being sure of what we hope for and certain of what we do not see." Hebrews 11:1, NIV

By faith, it is so, in Jesus name, *Amen.*

DAY 5

REFLECTION

God calls wives to submit to their husbands
and husbands to love their wives
as Jesus loved the church.

Submission in its truest form is a good thing. It's about a man loving, protecting, and providing. It's about a wife respecting and honoring him.

Understanding the role submission plays in your marriage is important for its success.

SCRIPTURE STUDY

For wives, this means submit to your husbands as to the Lord. For husbands, this means love your wives, just as Christ loved the church.

Ephesians 5: 22, 25

PRAYER

Heavenly Father, we recognize that we've allowed some things in our marriage to go unchecked.

Now they've become troublesome, working against us. We need help restoring order and establishing right alignment in our marriage.

We pray that you will give us the strength and power to be obedient to your instructions regarding the proper order of submission in marriage.

Renew our minds, so that we can receive your word in our hearts and follow your direction for how to live our lives.

By faith, it is so, in Jesus name, *Amen.*

DAY 6

REFLECTION

Again, submission is important to the structure and dynamic of a healthy marriage. The proper order of submission will help your marriage operate at its highest level. It consists of God's vision for order in marriage, it's a wonderful thing that you have no reason to be against.

Everyone submits in life. Man submits to God, wives submit to their husbands, children submit to their parents and so on.

SCRIPTURE STUDY

And further, submit to one another out of reverence for Christ.
Ephesians 5:21

PRAYER

God, you are our source for everything. Thank you for giving us a spirit of obedience in the place of rebellion regarding submission.

We understand that there is a process and proper order to everything you do.

Help us to be obedient to your word. We want our marriage to be healthy and successful.

Show us the ways that we can begin to implement the right behavior to change our habits in this area of our marriage.

Help us to be kind and loving to one another during this transition into right order.

By faith, it is so, in Jesus name, *Amen*.

DAY 7

REFLECTION

Don't fight submission. Remember, when God is involved in your marriage, you both have to submit to God first and foremost.

The biblical order of submission is a dynamic you must embrace.

The benefits of submission and being in right order according to God's word, is for your good. It's for the health of your marriage in the long run.

SCRIPTURE STUDY

No one has ever seen God. But if we love each other, God lives in us, and his love is brought to full expression in us.

1 John 4:12

PRAYER

God, we know you are with us. We desire to trust you completely. Help us get on the same page regarding submission for the benefit and health of our marriage. Increase our patience for what has become the intolerable.

Help us to trust in ourselves and our marriage again. God, reactivate our faith and renew our belief in miracles, signs and wonders, and in the impossible where our marriage is concerned.

We know that there is nothing too hard for you. God, we surrender our will to you. Have your way, Lord.

By faith, it is so, in Jesus name, *Amen.*

DAY 8

REFLECTION

Getting things in proper order will help get your marriage back on the right track. So again, remove any negative perception you might have had about what submission is.

Also, remember that it's never too late to change and get things going in the right direction. There is still hope.

SCRIPTURE STUDY

Love never gives up, never loses faith, is always hopeful, and endures through every circumstance.
1 Corinthians 13:7

PRAYER

God, thank you for this time of revelation and insight on where we have not gotten it right in our marriage.

Thank you for showing us how to rebuild our marriage foundation on you and how to re-align the order of leadership in our marriage.

We see now that at the core of submission is trust. We must first trust you as a unit to lead us. We must also trust each other again from the positions you've placed us in our marriage.

God, thank you that it's not too late.

By faith, it is so, in Jesus name, *Amen*.

THE GIFT OF
God's Love

DAY 9

REFLECTION

I want to encourage you to push through any anxiety or discomfort with this process so far. You have successfully completed over a week of praying every day for your marriage. It's only natural to feel some resistance to this new approach. Drawing nearer to God goes against your logic and desire to be in control of things. Don't worry. God has you. Trust Him. Keep going.

SCRIPTURE STUDY

Love keeps no records of wrongs.
1 Corinthians 13:4-5

PRAYER

God, you love us unconditionally. Thank you. We want to learn how to mimic your love for us in our marriage.

Your word says that love keeps no record of wrongs. Help us to let go of the memories of the wrongs we commit against each other.

We admit that this is difficult and easier said than done. We also know the more practice we have doing it, the better we will become at it. We have a choice that we can make each time. We will work to make the better choice of letting go and forgiving one another.

By faith, it is so, in Jesus name, *Amen.*

DAY 10

REFLECTION

The idea that God is going to change you, or your spouse's heart automatically is not accurate. You work in tandem with God by following the instructions He reveals to you during your prayer time.

Make sure your tuning into what God is revealing to you. Then do what He tells you to do to see the lasting results you desire to experience in your marriage.

SCRIPTURE STUDY

Love is patient. Love is kind.
1 Corinthians 13:4-5

PRAYER

God, bless us with the courage to follow your instructions for correcting our own behavior. We pray that the spirit of humility would cover our hearts and individual desires. We want to have harmony and peace in place of conflict. We surrender our individual wills for the betterment of our union.

We know that this is what you desire for us as well. Bless us with the wisdom to know when to yield to one another. Help us to lead with compassion and kindness toward each other instead of allowing disagreements to push us away from each other.

By faith, it is so, in Jesus name, *Amen*.

DAY 11

REFLECTION

You don't need to have all the answers right this minute. You just need to know the next right step to take. Ask God, "What do I need to do next? How do I approach this situation now and going forward?" Then listen for God to answer you in your spirit.

Resist the need to want to jump ahead of God. You'll have to repeat the lesson until it's learned. Better to practice patience with yourself and each other. Patience comes with practice.

SCRIPTURE STUDY

Love each other with genuine affection and take delight in honoring each other.

Romans 12:9-10

PRAYER

God, we pray that our faith doesn't fail during this process.

We've begun taking the steps you've shown us. We're working to rid ourselves of things that have taken root in our hearts that are causing us to be prideful and fearful.

We will choose to stay the course, even though we don't and won't know the outcome, before we obey.

God help us. Restore our ability to love one another freely.

By faith, it is so, in Jesus name, *Amen*.

DAY 12

REFLECTION

It's a process for a reason. You can only focus on doing one thing well at a time. Plus, the steps build upon one another and make the next one possible by faith. Your confidence in God builds with every step you take with Him.

Staying on God's path is a challenge. You must take it one day at a time. Focus only on the steps you need to take each day.

SCRIPTURE STUDY

Be kind to each other, tenderhearted, forgiving one another, just as God through Christ has forgiven you.
Ephesians 4:32

PRAYER

God, teach us how to value the things that matter to you.

We realize a lot of our conflict comes from unmet expectations and our lack of open communication with each other.

Help us to replace expectation with hope and gratitude. Show us how to change our minds regarding how we think things "should be" and allow room for adjustments to be made.

We rebuke the enemy in all his devices to seek to divide and tear apart that which you have brought together.

We are growing stronger in you every day.

By faith, it is so, in Jesus name, *Amen.*

DAY 13

REFLECTION

The closer your relationship is with God, the more you will see that things won't always make sense at first. God may direct you to do things that just don't add up in your mind.

Be careful not to give logic more power than what you feel in your spirit. Focus on being obedient and everything will work out for your good in the end.

SCRIPTURE STUDY

They say that God is passionate that the spirit he has placed within us should be faithful to him. And he gives grace generously. Come close to God, and God will come close to you.

James 4:5-6,8

PRAYER

God, open our eyes in the Spirit so that we can see beyond the surface of our relationship. Help us to resist the habit of glossing over deeper issues that are present. We realize we cannot begin to work on things until we shine light on the hidden issues within our hearts.

Give us the right words to say to each other so that we can be receptive and understanding toward one another. Help us to get out of our heads and use our hearts to deal with each other. Everything doesn't have to make sense. We speak life back into our relationship. Love and passion back into our hearts for one another.

By faith, it is so, in Jesus name, *Amen.*

DAY 14

REFLECTION

Direct communication, from a place of love, will allow your spouse to easily satisfy your needs and allow you to satisfy their needs in return.

Be transparent. Be respectful. Be open. Receive their words through the filter of love so that they're less likely to be distorted by fear and create hostility.

SCRIPTURE STUDY

Instead, we will speak the truth in love, growing in every way more and more like Christ, who is the head of his body, the church. He makes the whole body fit together perfectly. As each part does its own special work, it helps the other parts grow, so that the whole body is healthy, growing and full of love.

Ephesians 4:15-16

PRAYER

God, help us to fight through the frustration we feel within ourselves as the result of our own assumptions.

We will actively work on being clear about our needs and feelings. Our spouse won't have to guess. We don't want to create fear or confusion within our marriage.

Help us to be more sensitive toward each other at times when we're most vulnerable.

Work with us to reveal old issues that need to be addressed so we can resolve them.

We will speak to each other in love. We will work to listen to each other with love's ears. Show us the areas within us that are keeping us from receiving our spouse's words with love.

By faith, it is so, in Jesus name, *Amen*.

DAY 15

REFLECTION

God is clear in his word on how to show each other love. He wants you to do everything from a place of love.

Perfection is not the goal. You don't need to be perfect, to show each other love at all times. You must decide to.

Practice operating from a place of humility and determination for your part and allow God's grace to fill in the gaps when you fall short.

SCRIPTURE STUDY

My command is this: Love each other as I have loved you.
John 15:12

PRAYER

God, we humble ourselves before you. We need your wisdom to be successful in our marriage. We need to be able to discern the attacks of the enemy and fight him in the Spirit with your word.

We will not lose hope and be destroyed, we will have faith and be saved.

You know us better than we do. Help us connect to the depths of each other's hearts.

We pray for the ability to genuinely love one another. Perfect love cast out fear. Our love is made perfect in you.

By faith, it is so, in Jesus name, *Amen*.

DAY 16

REFLECTION

God is love. You and your spouse were created in the image of God, which means you both are love. Love is. No explanation needed.

Understand that everything you do in your marriage and in life should be done unto God. Take your focus off the other person. It's about your actions, attitude, and heart being right with God.

SCRIPTURE STUDY

God is love. Whoever lives in love lives in God, and God in them. This is how love is made complete among us so that we will have confidence on the day of judgment: In this world we are like Jesus. There is no fear in love.

1 John 4:16-18

PRAYER

Thank you, God, for being our example of unconditional love and tireless patience. We want to be expressions of your love toward us to each other.

Help us to see each other as extensions of you.

We desire to express love in everything we do. Help us to learn how to live this out in our everyday lives.

By faith, it is so, in Jesus name, *Amen*.

THE GIFT OF
God's Grace

DAY 17

REFLECTION

God uses certain situations to strengthen your faith and build up your confidence in Him. When your faith is tested you experience God in a whole new way. He shows up and once it's over you'll say, "It had to be God." You won't be able to give credit to anyone else but Him. That's why His instructions are going to sound crazy sometimes. No matter how crazy, hard, or confusing, trust God's plan and timing.

SCRIPTURE STUDY

"For I know the plans I have for you," says the Lord. "They are plans for good and not for disaster, to give you a future and a hope."

Jeremiah 29:11

PRAYER

God, we know that you are at work in our marriage. Even though we don't know all the details, we are doing our best to be obedient by faith.

Thank you for your presence and that we don't have to do this alone. Thank you that we can depend on you and trust you completely because your word says that you can do anything but fail.

God, we thank you that the work that we're doing on our marriage will be for your glory and honor. We resist the need to compare our in-progress to others finished work. We will keep our eyes fixed on you instead.

By faith, it is so, in Jesus name, *Amen.*

DAY 18

REFLECTION

God is in control and will equip you with everything you need to do his will. Take a deep breath. He has you, your spouse, and your marriage.

You're making progress. It might not feel like it or look like it on the surface. Remember, this is not about the outside. God is working internally to help you change and improve your character.

Continue to walk by faith, not by sight.

SCRIPTURE STUDY

Now faith is being sure of what I hope for and certain of what I do not see.

Hebrews 11: 1

He will equip us with everything to do his will.

Hebrews 13:21

PRAYER

God, thank you for growing and stretching our faith through the difficult times within our marriage.

You know what's best for us as a unit, even when we don't see eye-to-eye.

God, thank you for leading and guiding us in all truth. Thank you for your supernatural power to lead us by your Spirit, instead of us giving into our flesh and desires in the moment.

Thank you for the gift of hope. By faith, we will continue to speak things to come as though they are.

We're grateful that this process is helping us grow closer to each other and you.

By faith, it is so, in Jesus name, *Amen*.

DAY 19

REFLECTION

You've spent the last 18 days diligently seeking God in prayer and covering your marriage. Make sure you believe God for what you're praying for. This is faith mixed with hope in love. Believe and do not doubt. Remember, you're not responsible for the outcome. You're only responsible for doing your part. God will take care of the overall outcome.

SCRIPTURE STUDY

Without faith it is impossible to please God because those who come to Him must believe that He is and rewards those who diligently seek Him.

Hebrews 11:13

PRAYER

God, help us to raise our expectation. Disappointment and the trials of life have caused us to allow our faith to waver.

Show us how to believe for the impossible. We put our faith and trust in you and each other again.

We want to believe for the best out of ourselves, each other, and our marriage.

Thank you for keeping us this far. Thank you for the faith to believe in the miracles we're praying for, regarding us changing our hearts and bettering our relationship.

We want to please you first God. We will continue to seek you daily, knowing that in your right timing we will receive the answers to our prayers.

By faith, it is so, in Jesus name, *Amen*.

DAY 20

REFLECTION

Allow God to be whatever you need Him to be. Nothing is too hard for God. Realize that you are not alone in what you're going through. It's not easy and God knows this. He provides you with new grace every day that is enough to keep you through your circumstance. Keep your eyes on God and the bigger picture. Be encouraged.

SCRIPTURE STUDY

Consider it pure joy, my brother and sisters, whenever you face trials of many kinds, because you know that the testing of your faith produces perseverance. Let perseverance finish its work so that you may be mature and complete, not lacking anything.

James 1:2-4

PRAYER

God, you are our source for everything. We find everything we need in you.

Help us to find a balance within our marriage when things become overwhelming and more than we can handle.

We know that nothing is too hard for you. We release the things that have been weighing us down in our minds and spirits and caused us to doubt each other and our love.

Thank you for new grace every day. We desire to be mature and complete so that we're not lacking anything.

By faith, it is so, in Jesus name, *Amen.*

DAY 21

REFLECTION

Fatigue is natural. When you're in-process there is always a waiting period between where you are now and where you're going to end up.

The in-between is where distractions try to derail your progress. Constructively deal with any impatience. Stay the course. Stay focused on the result.

What you do in the in-between time will ultimately determine whether you're able to experience the blessings of God in your marriage.

SCRIPTURE STUDY

So, let's not get tired of doing what is good. At just the right time we will reap a harvest of blessing if we don't give up.
Galatians 6:9

PRAYER

God, help us to discipline ourselves during the waiting period. We don't want to rush the process and miss the lessons we need. You are strategic. There is a reason for every step we must take.

Help us to focus on what we have and where you're taking us. Our confidence is in you, not ourselves.

Strengthen us in our spirits so that we will not give up on the process, prematurely. Help us to resist reverting back to old behavior, meant to get us off course.

We will experience your blessings, God, in our marriage.

By faith, it is so, in Jesus name, *Amen.*

DAY 22

REFLECTION

There are no shortcuts with God. You need everything that God has for you.

God is not wasteful and there is purpose in everything He does. It is also for your own good and benefit.

God doesn't always change the situation. He changes you in the process and you're then able to change the situation.

SCRIPTURE STUDY

My grace is all you need. My power works best in weakness. So now I am glad to boast about my weaknesses, so that the power of Christ can work through me.

2 Corinthians 12:9

PRAYER

God, thank you that your grace is enough, and your strength is made perfect in our weakness. Help us to restore peace in our hearts and in our home.

We thank you for covering us in your love. We often find ourselves not knowing what to do in positions of weakness and times of uncertainty.

We need everything you have for us, God. Thank you for this time of pressing. We will give you all the glory and honor. Continue to show up and help us work through our issues.

By faith, it is so, in Jesus name, *Amen*.

DAY 23

REFLECTION

Every day that you draw closer to God, He'll reveal things within yourself and your marriage that need to be addressed.

As you continue this journey, know that it's not by your power that you're making these changes. It's God's power working in you and your spouse. Remember, it's worth it. God is faithful. He's going to exceed your expectations.

SCRIPTURE STUDY

Now to Him who is able to do above and beyond all that we ask or think according to the power that works in us- to Him be glory in the church and in Christ Jesus to all generations, forever and ever. Amen.
Ephesians 3:20-21

PRAYER

We're excited about our future, God. We're relieved that we're not relying on our strength but on your power working through us.

Thank you, God, for equipping us with everything we need daily to do your will. It's for our benefit and your glory. You want to bless us God. You want our marriage to be healthy, happy, flourishing, full of unconditional love, and affection.

It's all working out because you're in control. We're doing our part, God, and giving you something to bless.

Thank you for blowing our minds and rebuilding our foundation on you, which means you will continue to build us up in you.

By faith, it is so, in Jesus name, *Amen*.

DAY 24

REFLECTION

Gratitude and appreciation are important in any relationship.

Be thankful for this time, for your marriage, for your spouse, and for the process. When you do, you increase your capacity to receive even more blessings.

Everything might not be where it needs to be, but progress is being made every day. Celebrate the small steps, they too are miracles.

SCRIPTURE STUDY

However, as it is written: What no eye has seen, what no ear has heard, and what no human mind has conceived, are the things God has prepared for those who love him.

1 Corinthians 2:9

PRAYER

Thank you so much God for the gift of my spouse and marriage. We are grateful for your hearing our prayers back when we were single.

You have blessed our union. You want us to glorify you in our marriage by treating each other with love, especially, when no one else is watching.

We are accountable to you first God, and we do things unto you, so that you are pleased.

We are happy and grateful that our spouse benefits from our obedience to you.

We are grateful for the blessing of giving and receiving love through a human being. We will not curse what you have blessed us with.

By faith it is so, in Jesus name, *Amen*.

THE GIFT OF *Clean Hearts*

DAY 25

REFLECTION

It's important to identify any wall(s) you've built around your heart that's negatively impacting your marriage. Chances are if you have a wall up of any kind, toward your spouse, it's a result of something they've done that wasn't resolved.

Walls hinder love's ability to flow freely within your marriage. Walls also restrict your ability to give off positive, loving energy that's so beneficial to you and your marriage.

SCRIPTURE STUDY

Therefore, change your hearts and stop being stubborn.

Deuteronomy 10:16

PRAYER

God, we repent for having rebellious spirits, being defiant, and building walls that have restricted and choked the love from our hearts for each other.

We need you to help us see the errors of our ways. How we can work together to bring resolution to old issues. We want to resolve them, so that they don't further distance us from each other.

Show us how to remove the spirit of unforgiveness, which is hurting our relationship. We need you God to intercede on our behalf. We desire to share good, positive, loving energy toward each other daily.

By faith, it is so, in Jesus name, *Amen*.

DAY 26

REFLECTION

Decide to show your spouse unconditional love every day. Speak to them with love and respect, no matter what, even when you don't think they deserve it.

Work through any breakdown in communication. Quickly bring resolution to issues that cause you to not want to show them love.

It's your choice. It's a decision you get to make with each new day. Showing them love is a way you honor God's love.

SCRIPTURE STUDY

What you say flows from what is in your heart.
Luke 6:45

PRAYER

God, give us your words, thoughts, and intentions toward each other. Show us how to stop being blinded by our changing emotions. We want to handle our anger better.

Help us to release past hurt and pain caused by each other or created in our past.

We need ways to improve our loving communication in our marriage.

Your word says, "Life and death is in the power of the tongue." Help us God to use our words to build and edify one another. Tell us what steps we need to take to practice this all the time regardless of how we feel in the moment.

By faith, it is so, in Jesus name, *Amen*.

DAY 27

REFLECTION

To maintain a close personal relationship, you need more than rules–you need God's love in you.

Reset your mind. Focus on the reason why you should be love, have love, and speak love into your spouse. It's God.

SCRIPTURE STUDY

But now you must also rid yourselves of all such things as these: anger, rage, malice, slander, and filthy language from your lips. Do not lie to each other, since you have taken off your old self with its practices and have put on the new self, which is being renewed in knowledge in the image of its Creator.

Colossians 3:8-10

PRAYER

Thank you for this time of heart surgery, God. Even though painful, we trust you to show us how to become better versions of ourselves and to get us back centered on the things that are important to you and our marriage.

Thank you for caring enough about us and our marriage to correct us in our spirits when we're out of order. Thank you for giving us instructions and sound guidance through your word. Thank you for reminding us that above all we are new people in you and through our union.

We want our marriage to be love-filled.

By faith, it is so, in Jesus name. *Amen.*

DAY 28

REFLECTION

Anything you're holding onto in silence is turning toxic. You can pretend for a while that it's "nothing", but "nothing" grows. Communicate your feelings in a loving manner. Allow your spouse to do the same. Then listen from a place of empathy and love for your spouse.

Sometimes, it's necessary to put your need to be right and heard on the back burner for the benefit of harmony and peace within your relationship.

SCRIPTURE STUDY

And don't sin by letting anger control you. Don't let the sun go down while you are still angry, for anger gives a foothold to the devil.

Ephesians 4:26-27

PRAYER

We are seeking you, God. Not because we must, but because we've decided to, out of love and reverence for you and who you are.

We pray that this will duplicate in our marriage. We want to be better partners. Our marriage is secure in you and will grow and flourish in right order.

Thank you for increasing our patience and love for each other during this time of correction and revelation.

By faith, it is so, in Jesus name, *Amen*.

DAY 29

REFLECTION

Anytime you find yourself in or being pushed into a negative place, stop and pray. Calm your spirit and check your energy. Avoid transferring the negative energy and having it cause an issue with your spouse. Lead with gentleness, kindness, forgiveness, and patience.

SCRIPTURE STUDY

Therefore, as God's chosen people, holy and dearly loved, clothe yourselves with compassion, kindness, humility, gentleness and patience. Bear with each other and forgive one another if any of you has a grievance against someone. Forgive as the Lord forgave you. And over all these virtues put on love, which binds them all together in perfect unity.

Colossians 3:12-14

PRAYER

God, show us what it means to have the hearts of servants.

We know we don't and won't get it right all the time. However, we desire to limit the times where we are at odds with each other.

Help us to be more forgiving and how to show grace to one another the same way you offer us grace when we fall short.

Teach us how to be lighthearted.

Bless us with enough courage to admit when we are wrong and seek resolution quickly, so anger doesn't linger and grow.

By faith, it is so, in Jesus name, *Amen.*

DAY 30

REFLECTION

Continue to be patient with yourself and your spouse during this process. It's not about perfection. It's about progress. Things won't change overnight. With that said, I want to remind you that your spouse and your marriage are both blessings from God. You have a duty to honor the blessing God has entrusted you with. Pour love into one another.

SCRIPTURE STUDY

Always be humble and gentle. Be patient with each other, making allowance for each other's faults because of your love. Make every effort to keep yourselves united in the Spirit, binding yourselves together with peace.

Ephesians 4:2-3

PRAYER

Thank you, God, for keeping our marriage during the times of our self-created chaos. Thank you for helping us increase our patience with each other and with the everyday issues of life.

We are reminded in your word how our marriage is a blessing from you and how you want us to honor you with how we treat each other.

We will continue to seek your wisdom and to follow the instructions you are giving us. We know that this process will take time. We won't focus on the outcome, but on the steps we're able to take every day to improve.

By faith, it is so, in Jesus name, *Amen.*

DAY 31

REFLECTION

Continue to see your marriage as a gift. Put your best foot forward. Decide to do what's needed to make it work. Focus on what you can control, YOU.

If you want encouragement, love, and support, treat your spouse accordingly. It's important that both of you really get on the same page. You both must recognize what needs to happen in your marriage, specifically, to get it to a higher level and happier place.

SCRIPTURE STUDY

Let love be your highest goal!
1 Corinthians 14:1

PRAYER

God, thank you for blessing us with each other. Thank you for hearing our prayers.

Help us to continue to see our marriage as the blessing that it is. Thank you that we can choose to release feelings of resentment, unforgiveness, and lack of trust toward one another.

Reveal the root of our anger, so that it's not acted out against each other. Show us how best to reach resolution as quickly as possible.

We want to live in peace together. We want love to be our highest goal.

By faith, it is so, in Jesus name, *Amen.*

DAY 32

REFLECTION

Love is more than a feeling. It's a decision you make to serve another's interest over your own.

Only with God's help can you love another person "with all your heart."

SCRIPTURE STUDY

And whatever you do or say, do it as a representative of the Lord Jesus, giving thanks through him to God the Father.
Colossians 3:17

PRAYER

God, we need your help with loving each other "with all our heart." We want to be able to express love toward our spouse. We want to show them love even when we don't feel loving and even when we don't feel they are deserving of our love.

Deliver us from being controlled by our emotions. Lead us by your Spirit, God, and help us to choose obedience over sacrifice in all that we do.

Help us to follow your example of what it means to love. We don't want to take each other for granted.

By faith, it is so, in Jesus name, *Amen*.

THE GIFT OF *Intimacy*

DAY 33

REFLECTION

Intimacy and sex are not the same things. It's true that sex falls under the umbrella of intimacy, however, there are many non-sexual ways to be intimate.

Each partner needs to be willing to learn and value the ways that your spouse desires to be fulfilled intimately. It's important that there be a healthy balance of sexual and non-sexual intimacy.

SCRIPTURE STUDY

Now the man and his wife were both naked, but they felt no shame.
Genesis 2:25

PRAYER

God, help us to be open to explore and discover the different ways we need to give and receive love from each other.

We want to be fulfilled both sexually and non-sexually within our marriage.

Give us the desire and patience to learn each other again for the first time.

Help us to reprioritize each other and intimacy in our relationship. Show us how to deeply connect through our dedicated time that leaves us both fulfilled and feeling appreciated.

Give us the right words to speak that edify and arouse our hearts and desire for one another.

By faith, it is so, in Jesus name, *Amen*.

DAY 34

REFLECTION

Open communication, being present, listening, undistracted to your spouse, offering support and encouragement, and sharing positive energy are all ways of engaging them intimately.

Intimacy is defined as closeness, togetherness, affection, or an act of intimacy. The above acts of intimacy require you to take time out to devote your attention to one another. Trust and confidence are built on the foundation of spending intimate time together.

SCRIPTURE STUDY

Most important of all, continue to show deep love for each other, for love covers a multitude of sins.

1 Peter 4:8

PRAYER

God, we need to do better at the little things. We've allowed life to distract us to the point of neglecting each other.

I pray that you'll continue to show us the way back to each other both physically and emotionally.

We both want to be confident in our relationship and close in our marriage. However, we realize, we must begin to prioritize our relationship and each other, so that our bond can continue to be strengthened, not weakened by absence.

Help us to begin by making small changes over time that will help.

By faith, it is so, in Jesus name, *Amen*.

DAY 35

REFLECTION

Sex is an important part of a healthy marriage. It's important for both of you to be satisfied and to get what you desire sexually. Lack of sex and a lack of sexual pleasure create a lot of rifts and a lot of conflict in marriages. Be open and willing to talk about sex with each other. This way you're both more confident on how to please one another, sexually.

SCRIPTURE STUDY

Do not deprive each other of sexual relations, unless you both agree to refrain from sexual intimacy for a limited time, so you can give yourselves more completely to prayer. Afterward, you should come together again so that Satan won't tempt you because of your lack of self-control.

1 Corinthians 7: 5

PRAYER

God, remove any wrong-thinking we have developed from outside influences that have caused us to limit our willingness to be sexually intimate.

One of the blessings of marriage is sex with your partner. Sex is an act of intimacy that you have given us as a gift for our pleasure.

Help us to be open and honest with each other about the causes or issues that are keeping us from fulfilling one another in this area of intimacy.

Show us how to be sensitive to each other's needs. Facilitate healing of any brokenness in this area, God.

By faith, it is so, in Jesus name, *Amen*.

DAY 36

REFLECTION

Communication is a part of great sex. When you openly communicate in this area, you're showing your desire to pleasure your partner intimately. This creates an environment for more pleasurable sex for the both of you, which is the point.

When you both are working together to create an amazing sexual relationship, you're going to strengthen your marriage. There'll be less to fight about. You're both going to be happier.

SCRIPTURE STUDY

Love each other with genuine affection and take delight in honoring each other.
Romans 12:10

PRAYER

God, we now know how important communication is to our sex life and is itself a form of intimacy.

We recognize that we need work in this area. Help us not to assume, take things personally, or be oversensitive toward each other when we communicate.

Help us to be better listeners and to be open to follow our spouse's instructions and directions. Rid us of selfishness and the need to be in control.

Continue to work with us on our willingness to submit to each other out of obedience to you.

By faith, it is so, in Jesus name, *Amen*.

DAY 37

REFLECTION

Sex shouldn't be used as a weapon. It's not meant for you to use for revenge or to punish in any way.

If you're withdrawing the things your partner needs as some sort of punishment it will eventually backfire.

That's not the way to go about it. If there's a problem, talk about it. Especially, when it comes to sex.

SCRIPTURE STUDY

There is no fear in love, but perfect love drives out fear, because fear involves punishment. The one who fears has not been perfected in love.

1 John 4:18

PRAYER

God, thank you for opening our eyes to the ways we might have misused the gift of sex within our marriage in the past. To punish or hurt instead of to give and receive pleasure and express our love.

Show us how to restore our sexual relationship back to its original intent within our marriage. We ask for forgiveness and repent for wrong motives where this is concerned.

Going forward, we will work to communicate better to avoid or quickly resolve misunderstandings in other areas of our relationship. We don't want them to carry over and disrupt our times of intimacy.

By faith, it is so, in Jesus name, *Amen.*

DAY 38

REFLECTION

Sex in marriage should consistently be a learning process. You must continuously reintroduce yourselves to each other. Whatever you all decide on; the key is to be consistent.

Enjoy each other as much and as often as possible. Praise each other's performance and practice constructively criticizing each other as well. Doing both will ensure that you both stay pleased and satisfied in your sexual relationship.

SCRIPTURE STUDY

---

*My beloved is mine, and I am his …*Song of Solomon 2:16
… Put me like a seal over your heart, like a seal on your arm. For love is as strong as death.
Song of Solomon 8:6

PRAYER

God, help us not to become rigid in our behavior and thoughts. You desire us to keep a zest and curiosity for life and for love. This also applies to each other, our marriage, and our sex life.

Help us to find ways to maintain our physical and sexual attraction toward one another. One of the many benefits of marriage is sexual relations without guilt or shame.

We want our attraction to be new each day. We want to continue to encourage each other in love so that fear or reservations won't hinder our intimate relationship.

By faith, it is so, in Jesus name, *Amen*.

DAY 39

REFLECTION

The ways you and your spouse practice intimacy within your relationship will need to be adjusted over time.

It's natural for you to develop different tastes and want to try new things. It's healthy. Be flexible with each other and continue to use the intimacy of communication to stay on the same page.

Remember, intimacy and sex are both acts of love that should be shared and experienced freely within your marriage.

SCRIPTURE STUDY

Love flashes like fire, the brightest kind of flame.
Many waters cannot quench love,
nor can rivers drown it.
Song of Solomon 8:6-7

PRAYER

God, help us to connect to each other in ways that even we don't know we'd like to be accessed. You know us in the most intimate way. Help us to learn each other the way you know us.

Guide us in our intimacy with each other the way that only you can, God.

We want our love to consume us, purify us, and cleanse us of the past and the future so that we can fully experience each other completely in every moment.

Help us to honor each other by not taking each other for granted in any area.

By faith, it is so, in Jesus name, *Amen*.

DAY 40

REFLECTION

The marriage bed is undefined. I'm not here to define what's acceptable or not acceptable within your marriage and sex life. I'm here to stress the need to be on the same page with each other. That requires a mutual effort, patience, and understanding.

SCRIPTURE STUDY

The husband should fulfill his wife's sexual needs, and the wife should fulfill her husband's needs. The wife gives authority over her body to her husband, and the husband gives authority over his body to his wife.

1 Corinthians 7: 3-4

PRAYER

God, prayer is also a form of intimacy with you and each other. Thank you for helping us get back on the same page in major areas within our marriage.

We pray that our renewed minds, changed hearts, and closer connection will stay intact. We will continue to keep each other lifted in prayer and stay close to you in our relationship.

God, thank you for teaching us how to better relate to each other, love each other, and recreate intimacy in our marriage over the last 40 days.

We seal our love in you. Thank you for the hedge of protection that guards our hearts and minds in Christ Jesus.

By faith, it is so, in Jesus name, *Amen.*

CONCLUSION

But 'God made them male and female' from the beginning of creation. 'This explains why a man leaves his father and mother and is joined to his wife, and the two are united into one.' Since they are no longer two but one, let no one split apart what God has joined together.

Mark 10:6-9 (NLT)

ABOUT THE AUTHOR

Stephan Labossiere is *the* "Relationship Guy." An authority on real love, real talk, real relationships. The brand *Stephan Speaks* is synonymous with happier relationships and healthier people around the globe. For more than a decade, Stephan has committed himself to breaking down relationship barriers, pushing past common facades, and exposing the truth. It is his understanding of REAL relationships that has empowered millions of people, clients and readers alike, to create their best lives by being able to experience and sustain greater love.

Seen, heard, and chronicled in national and international media outlets including; the *Tom Joyner Morning Show, The Examiner, ABC*, GQ, and *Huffington Post Live*. The certified life & relationship coach, speaker, and award winning, bestselling author is the voice that the world tunes into for answers to their difficult relationship woes. From understanding the opposite sex, to navigating the paths and avoiding the pitfalls of relationships and self-growth, Stephan's relationship advice and insight helps countless men and women overcome the situations hindering them from achieving an authentically amazing life.

Stephan is highly sought-after because he is able to dispel the myths of relationship breakdowns and obstacles–platonic, romantic, and otherwise—with fervor and finesse. His signature style, relatability, and passion make international audiences sit up and pay attention.

"My message is simple: life and relationships require truth. The willingness to speak truth and the bravery to acknowledge truth is paramount."

Are you listening?

Enough said.

POPULAR BOOKS BY *Stephan Speaks*

www.BetterMarriageBetterLoving.com

www.GetAManToCherishYou.com

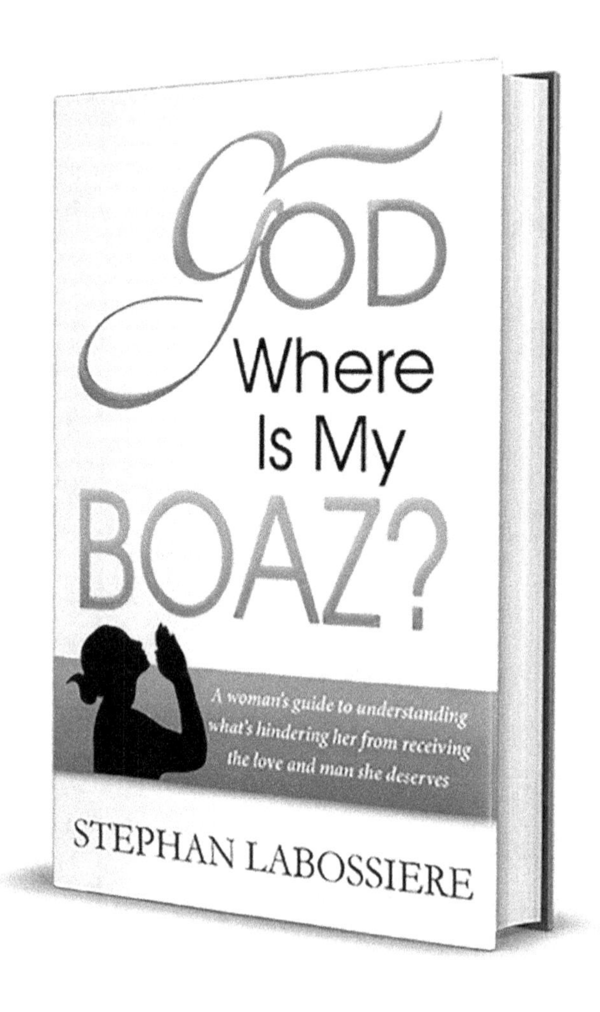

www.GodWhereIsMyBoaz.com

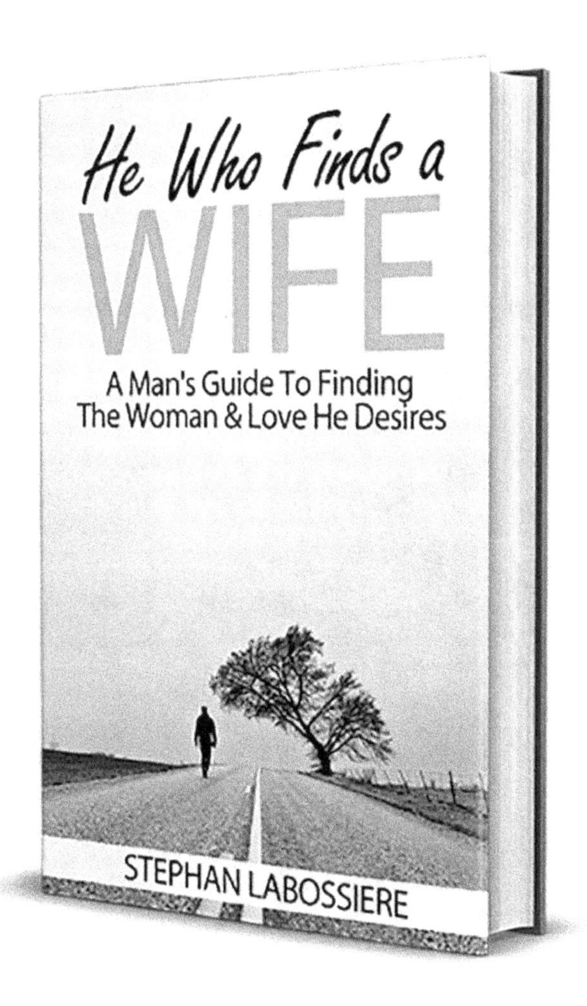

www.HeWhoFinds.com

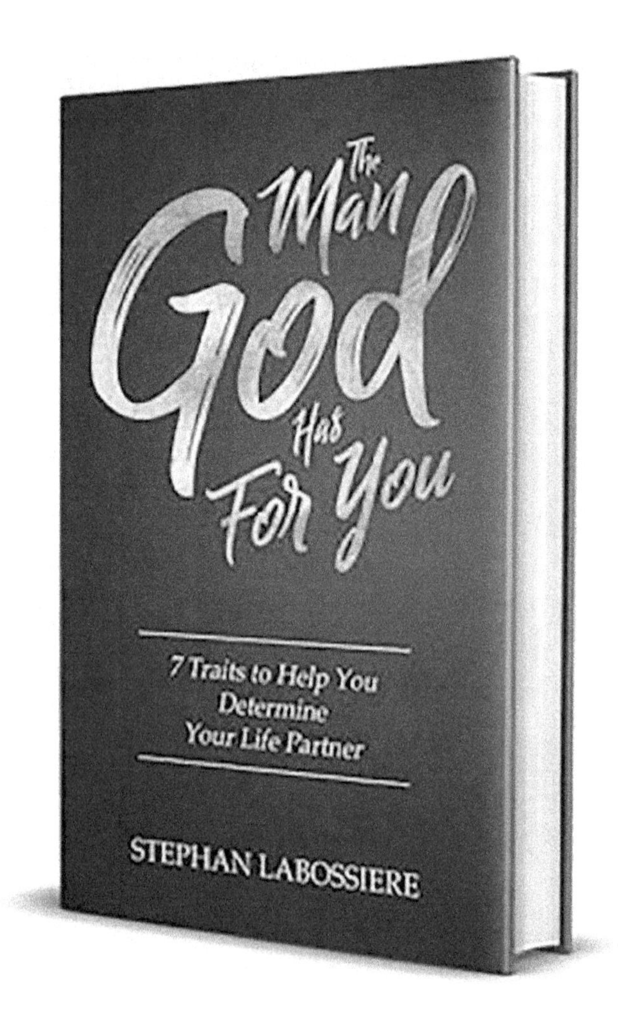

www.TheManGodHasForMe.com

WHAT CLIENTS & READERS ARE SAYING ABOUT *Stephan Speaks!*

INSIGHT & HONESTY

Stephan Labossiere has a rare blend of compassion, insight and honesty. He understands relationships, and is a supportive partner and guide on your journey to creating the love and life you want.

–Lisa Marie Bobby

HE'S FUN & LOVING

You hear people saying you must love yourself first, so you can attract the love of your life. This is what I wanted, and for me I did not quite know what this meant until I worked with Stephan. His work is fun, he is very loving, and you get results fast, because he sees very clearly what is going on. I truly recommend signing up for his coaching!

–Dominique, *Paris, France*

continued

A JOY TO WORK WITH

As someone who has studied the role of men and women in relationships in our society for many years, it has been a joy to get to know and work with Stephan. His knowledge and candid from the heart writings and speaking on the topic of relationships are a breath of fresh air and sure to take you and your relationships to a more authentic and loving way of being.

–Tom Preston

More relationship resources can be found at
www.StephanSpeaks.com/shop/

You can also follow me on
Twitter & Instagram: **@StephanSpeaks**
or find me on Facebook under
"Stephan Speaks Relationships"

CPSIA information can be obtained
at www.ICGtesting.com
Printed in the USA
FSHW011203210121

9 780998 018928